Note

Ahoy, pirates! Set your sails for the open seas, and keep your eye out for buried treasure and enemy ships! And don't forget to bring along this little book, which is packed with challenging mazes, word searches, crosswords, and find-the-differences, among other puzzles. Join in the excitement of a battle at sea, as well as searching for hidden gold and pirate swords.

There are 48 pages of puzzles to enjoy. Do your best to solve them all, but if you need help with the answers, you can turn to the Solutions section beginning on page 53. When you have finished the puzzles, you can have even more fun coloring in the pictures with colored pencils, crayons, or markers. Now grab your pirate hat—we're ready to set sail!

Help the pirates count their pieces of gold. Then circle the treasure chest with that number.

Use the letters in the pirate's greeting to spell out the answers to the clues.

Here are the famous "Swashbuckling Seven"! Put an X over the two pirates who look different from the Swashbucklers.

7

Swab, swab, swab the _____,
Mopping is not _____ ...
And just like
All my other _____
I can't wait 'til it's _____!

done
deck
chores
fun

Use the words in the puddles on the deck to finish the pirate's song.

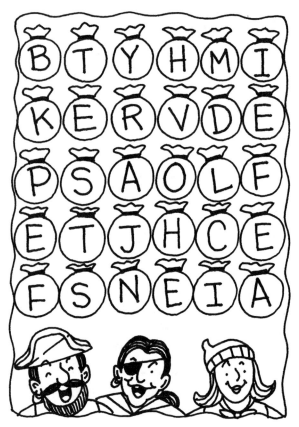

Cross out the first bag of loot. Then cross out every other bag. The letters that are left spell out another name for "pirates."

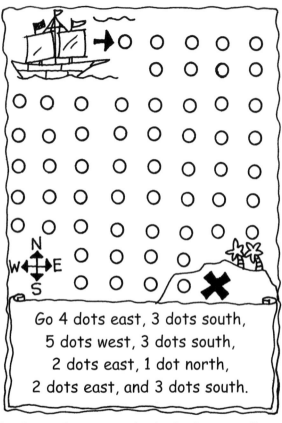

Go 4 dots east, 3 dots south,
5 dots west, 3 dots south,
2 dots east, 1 dot north,
2 dots east, and 3 dots south.

Starting at the arrow, color in the dots according to the directions and you'll end up at buried treasure!

While this pirate reads his map, look carefully and circle five things that are wrong in the picture.

The life of a pirate is so exciting! Find and color in the letters that spell "ADVENTURE."

12

Notorious Nate is well known on the high seas. Look carefully and draw his other half, so he can board his ship.

vheosl

_ _ _ _ _ _

pma

_ _ _

pelsecote

_ _ _ _ _ _ _ _ _

epro

_ _ _ _

Use the picture clues to unscramble the words—you will discover what the ship's crew is taking on their next voyage.

14

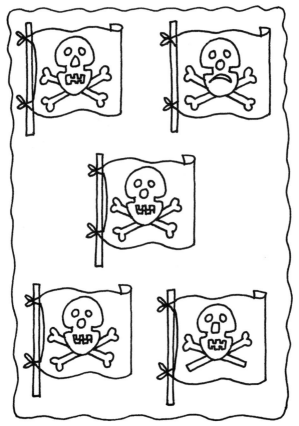

Take a close look at these pirate flags. Circle the two flags that are exactly the same.

This grumpy pirate loves to say, "Aargh"! Count how many times he has said it and write the number in the bubble next to the parrot.

16

Here is a picture of Blackbeard the Pirate. Use the letter code to color in the picture. Color the frame, too!

17

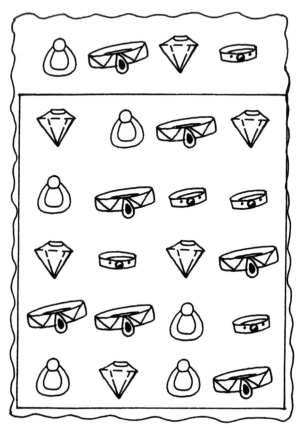

Four pieces of pirate jewels are shown at the top. Find and circle another row of these four jewels in the box. Look across, down, and on the diagonal.

18

```
L N L D L N
N L A N D D
L A N D L N
D A D L D A
L L A N D L
```

This pirate is on the lookout for land! Searching up, down, and across, find and circle the word "LAND" five times.

Here's a happy pirate with his treasure chest.

This looks like the same picture, but it's not! Find and circle the five things that have changed.

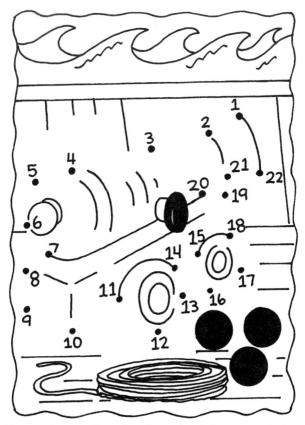

Do you know where the pirates load the cannonballs?
Connect the dots from 1 to 22 to find out.

Color 1 ▽ yellow.
Color 2 □'s red.
Color 3 △'s blue.
Color 4 ▭'s green.
Color 5 O's purple.

This pirate ship is made of many shapes. Find the color that matches each shape and color in the ship.

Write the letter that begins each picture clue. You will spell out the name of a famous pirate.

These swords were hidden in a pirate ship. Find the longest sword and circle it. Find the shortest sword and draw a line under it.

25

nest

lip

carrot

Look at the picture clues on the left. Draw a line from each picture to the word it rhymes with on the right.

How many in the air?____
How many on the deck?____
How many all together?____

Some pirates are shooting cannonballs to scare off their enemies. Count the cannonballs and answer the questions.

Look closely at the outline of each pirate hat. Then draw a line to the hat that matches the outline.

28

Storm clouds are brewing! Find and shade in an ice cream cone, a spoon, a baseball cap, a sword, a crescent moon, and a hamburger.

BURIED TREASURE!

BEE DUST
SIR
STRIPE RAISE
TREE RAIL
CUB SEA EAT
TIME RAT
SIT DRY BIRD

Cross out any word on the treasure chest that cannot be made from the letters in "BURIED TREASURE." How many words are left? Write the number on the shovel.

30

These pirates have found buried treasure and are celebrating. Match each happy pirate to his or her shadow.

Finish drawing the second, third, and fourth flags so that they look just like the first flag (the one with the arrow pointing to it).

Use the number code to discover why Dizzy Dave can't go on the next pirate voyage. Write the letters in the blanks.

S [ ] INY

VAL [ ] ABLE

COI [ ] S and

LOO [ ] !

The captain is telling the crew what they will be searching for. Write the word "HUNT" in the boxes from top to bottom to find out his message.

34

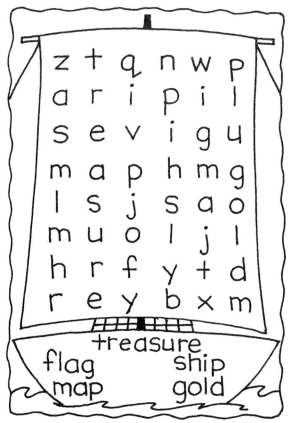

z t q n w p
a r i p i l
s e v i g u
m a p h m g
l s j s a o
m u o l j l
h r f y t d
r e y b x m

treasure
flag   ship
map   gold

Read the pirate words written on the ship. Then find and circle each word on the sail. Look across, down, and on the diagonal.

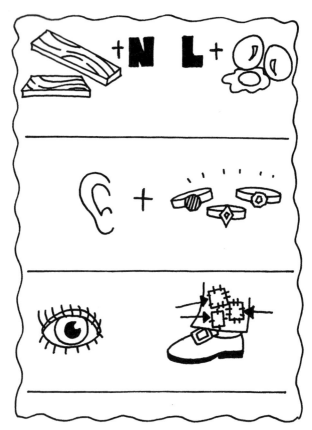

On each line, write the words that go with the pictures. Then you will find out three things that pirates are known for!

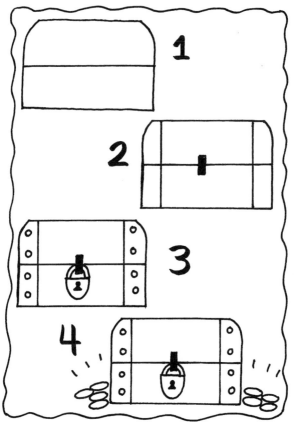

It's easy to draw a picture of a treasure chest. Just follow the four steps on this page.

Pirates use powder kegs during a battle. Count the powder kegs and underline that number on one of the ship's sails.

_ ank

_ ank

_ ank

a b c d e f g h i
j k l m n o p q
r s t u v w x y z

Complete the words on the ship's planks by using three letters that are together in the alphabet.

It's time to "drop anchor" for the night. Draw a path that will take the anchor all the way down to the bottom of the sea.

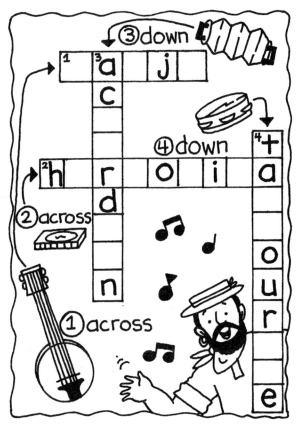

Pirates love to play music! Use the picture clues to fill in the names of four musical instruments in the puzzle. Some letters have been added to get you started.

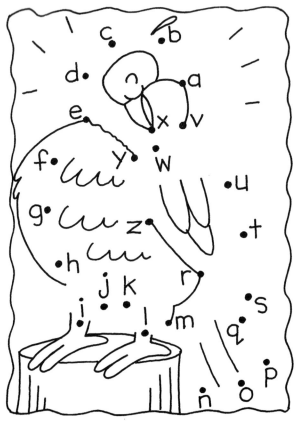

Captain Crawford always carries his favorite pet on his shoulder. Connect the dots in alphabetical order to see its picture.

42

Draw the correct number of jewels to add up to the total on each bag of loot.

These pirates are firing the cannon to protect their ship during a battle at sea.

44

But look again! Find and circle the six things that have changed in the picture.

Find the parts of this picture that have a solid black dot in them. Then shade in these parts and you will see what steers the pirate ship!

46

Here are some shells that the pirates will see when they reach the shore. Count the number of shells for each type and write the number in the space under the arrow.

riches and fame

1. _____
2. _____
3. _____
4. _____
5. _____
6. _____
7. _____
8. _____
9. _____
10. _____
11. _____
12. _____
13. _____
14. _____

Some things that make pirates happy are riches and fame. Using the words "RICHES AND FAME," make as many new words as possible. You can use a sheet of paper, too.

48

"X" marks the spot! Draw a path from each pirate at the bottom to see who will reach the buried treasure at the "X" first!

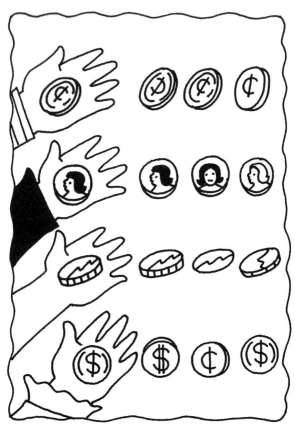

Circle the coin in each row that matches the coin in each pirate's hand.

Use the clues at the top to decide which map will lead the pirates to the gold. Put a check mark on that map.

The pirates have left a secret message for you! Write
the letter that comes before each letter below a blank.
Use the alphabet in the bottle for help. Good luck!

Solutions

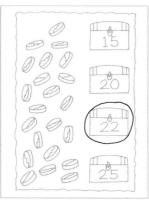

page 5

page 6

page 7

page 8

54

page 9

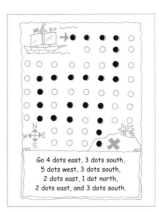

Go 4 dots east, 3 dots south,
5 dots west, 3 dots south,
2 dots east, 1 dot north,
2 dots east, and 3 dots south.

page 10

page 11

page 12

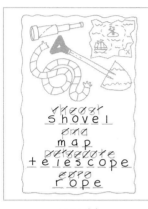

page 14

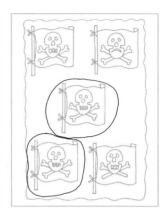

page 15

page 16

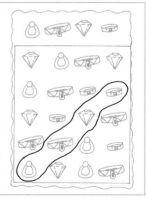

page 18

page 19

page 21

page 22

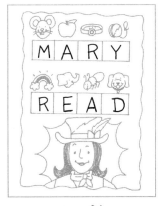

page 24

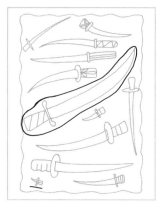

page 25

nest

lip

carrot

page 26

How many in the air? 14
How many on the deck? 7
How many all together? 21

page 27

page 28

page 29

page 30

page 31

page 32

page 33

page 34

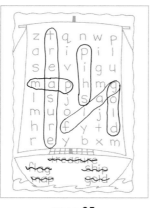

page 35

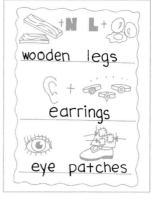

page 36

page 38

page 39

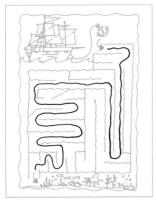

page 40

page 41

page 42

page 43

page 45

page 46

page 47

riches and fame

possible answers:

1. man
2. ran
3. farm
4. came
5. march
6. hand
7. send
8. find
9. same
10. car
11. seed
12. mean
13. near
14. deer

page 48

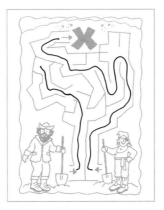

page 49

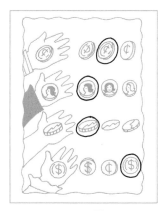

page 50

page 51

page 52